Beware the Morris Minor

John Townsend

SPRINGFIELD
SCHOOL
PORTSMOUTH

ENGLISH
DEPARTMENT

Stanley Thornes (Publishers) Ltd

© John Townsend 1983

All rights reserved. No part of this publication may be reproduced or transmitted in any form or by any means, electronic or mechanical, including photocopy, recording, or any information storage and retrieval system, without permission in writing from the publisher or under licence from the Copyright Licensing Agency Limited. Further details of such licences (for reprographic reproduction) may be obtained from the Copyright Licensing Agency Limited, of 90 Tottenham Court Road, London W1P 9HE.

First published in 1983 by Hutchinson Education
Reprinted in 1985, 1988, 1989

Reprinted in 1992 by
Stanley Thornes (Publishers) Ltd
Ellenborough House
Wellington Street
CHELTENHAM GL50 1YD
England

Reprinted 1994

British Library Cataloguing in Publication Data

Townsend, John, *1924–*
  Beware the Morris Minor.—(Spiral series)
  I. Title
  423′.914[J]   PZ7

  ISBN 0 7487 1046 9

Cover photograph by Steve Richards
Cover design by Martin Grant-Hudson
Printed and bound in Great Britain at Martin's The Printers, Berwick

1

You probably won't believe this. I don't blame you in a way. Even I think it is absurd, yet I know what has happened. There is no more I can do now. You see, something dreadful is about to happen — something you might not think possible. I am frightened. You would be too, and it's all because of a car. You must try to understand. I must try to explain. It is all I can do now. There is nothing else left. Nothing.

It had to end this way. It was all too good to be true. Now I must pay the price. You will soon see what I mean. You will soon see why I am scared. I am not ill, at least, not really. I am not mad. I am not even old. Today is my birthday. I am thirty. I am going to die on my thirtieth birthday. I have just made a phone call. That is how I know. You will soon see what I mean.

I must go back to the beginning and that means I must start with my car. That's what all this is about. My car and me. Although I didn't know it at the time, it was odd from the very start. When I first got my car there was something strange about it. It was only later I began to realize what it was.

2

When I was seventeen my Uncle Bob said he would teach me to drive. I was very keen on the idea. He had a Morris Minor. It was blue. It was a good little car. I took to it straight away. I drove it easily. Whenever Uncle Bob took me out I could drive it straight away. There was nothing to it. He said it suited me. He took a photograph of me sitting on the bonnet.

After a while, my uncle thought I was ready to take my driving test. 'You can take it in my car,' he said. 'You get on well with the Morris. You should pass.' I was very grateful.

My driving test went well. It was a piece of cake. In fact, now I think of it, it was then that I first noticed something unusual, something strange about the old Morris Minor. I didn't have to think about the test. The car seemed to do everything just right. I passed without any trouble at all.

Straight after the test I took off the 'L' plates and drove back to Uncle Bob's house. I was really pleased. He would be happy too. I was grateful to him for teaching me to drive so well.

I parked the car outside his house and went to the

front door. I was going to tear up the 'L' plates in front of him to show him I had passed. That was what I planned to do, but something was wrong.

My Auntie Sue answered the door. She was upset. 'Bob was taken ill,' she said, 'He had to go into hospital very suddenly.' I thought she was going to cry. I was upset too. I wanted to tell him I had passed my test. 'Come round tomorrow and see what the news is,' she said. She told me I could borrow Uncle Bob's car for the night. 'You can drive it home on your own now,' she said, 'Bob won't be needing it for a few days.' It was kind of her.

It was strange driving on my own. I had never driven the car without anyone beside me before. I decided to go for a drive around the town. I had really got used to the Morris Minor. I would have to think about buying my own car now. I would have to save up a lot of money. I drove back home. Suddenly the engine started coughing and spluttering. I didn't know what to do. Then the engine stopped. I couldn't start it. In the end I had to phone a garage and they towed the Morris away.

3

Auntie Sue said I could keep the Morris Minor until Uncle Bob came out of hospital. That was kind of her. In fact it was still at the garage. A lot of work needed to be done on it. I didn't know how I was going to pay for it. I hoped Uncle Bob would give me the money.

They wanted to keep the car at the garage for a few days. It needed a lot of new parts and probably a new engine. I phoned them up on Friday afternoon at three o'clock to see if it was ready. The mechanic said they had just that minute finished work on the Morris and it was as good as new. I was pleased. Uncle Bob would be pleased with the new engine. It would be even better now. He might not like the cost. I thought I would help pay some of it. I walked to the garage and collected the car. I just about managed to pay. It cost a lot. Then I drove the car home and put it inside the garage.

Just before I went to bed, the phone rang. It was my Auntie Sue. Uncle Bob had died in hospital that afternoon. She said I could keep his car. That was what he would have wanted. I didn't know what to say. I was really upset. I told Auntie Sue how sorry

I was. 'When did he die?' I asked. It was at three o'clock that afternoon.

4

I was shocked. We were all shocked. It was so sudden. Even the doctors didn't seem to know what was wrong. Uncle Bob seemed fine the last time I saw him. It was odd. Now the car was mine, my own Morris Minor. Of course I was pleased. I couldn't afford to buy my own car. Now I owned my own blue Morris Minor. It was strange, though. I mean, it is queer driving a dead man's car, especially Uncle Bob's — especially after the strange way he died. It was all so sudden.

I was really going to take care of that car. I owed it to Uncle Bob. I would never part with it. At least, that's what I told myself then. It was in good condition and I was going to make sure it stayed that way.

It is funny really. I had always been a clumsy person. You could say I was accident prone. Things often went wrong for me. I had never done very well at school. I had never passed an exam in my life. Yet I passed that driving test with no trouble at all. It was easy. I didn't have to try. Somehow I knew I would pass. Ever since I sat in that car, things seemed to improve. I had no more clumsy accidents, no more mistakes, no more bad luck. It was then I first realized there was something special about the car. Was the Morris Minor like a lucky charm? Did it bring me good luck? It was more than that. There was something else. I didn't notice it for a while. There was something odd about my Morris Minor. There was something different about me. You'll soon see what I mean.

5

The years went by. The blue Morris Minor was still
my pride and joy. I kept it clean. I always polished
it. It was a good car. Nothing ever went wrong
with it. I hardly ever had to look under the bonnet.
Nothing needed doing to the engine. It was always
reliable.

The first time anything went wrong, it made me
think. It made me worry. There really was
something odd about it.

One evening I was driving the Morris through town.
I was going to see Auntie Sue. She had moved and
now lived a few miles away. We still kept in touch.
She always asked me about the car. She wanted to
hear all my news.

I was turning the corner into her road when the car
suddenly stopped. It was so sudden that the car
behind screeched to a halt. It was too late. It
didn't have time to stop. It crashed into the back
of my Morris Minor. It hit the bumper with a crack.
I felt a dreadful pain at the base of my spine.

The next thing I knew there was a man at my car
door trying to pull me out. He was wild. He was
furious. He thought I did it on purpose. It wasn't

even my fault. I got out and tried to explain but he was mad. The next thing happened so quickly. He hit me. Not once, but twice — hard thumps in my face. Two mad thumps — one straight on my nose, the other right on my left eye. I was dazed.

The next thing was, he stormed off. He slammed his door and drove off at top speed. I ran to look at my back bumper. I thought it would be dented, but it was just fine. No damage at all. I was still shocked, not from the pain from his thumps — but the lack of it. I didn't feel it at all. I couldn't feel a thing. All I could feel was the pain in my back. It was odd. He had really thumped my nose and left eye but there was no pain, no mark. Nothing.

I got back in the car and drove up to Auntie Sue's. It was only when I walked up her drive that I saw how odd it all was. I had been hit hard in the face twice but I was fine. When I looked at the car I just couldn't believe it. The other car had crashed into my back bumper. There had been nothing in front of me. How then did my Morris Minor get a dented bonnet with a leaking radiator? Water was splashing out on to the road. That was not all. The left head lamp was smashed.

6

The car was repaired. The head lamp was fixed and the bonnet straightened out. My back ache went too. I was surprised. This was the first bit of bad luck I had known since I had the Morris Minor. It was all rather strange. I had driven the car for several years now and that was the only trouble I had known. At least, that was until the next time.

It was odd how I hadn't realized sooner. Since I'd had that car I had never been ill, not even with a cold. I hadn't thought about it until people kept saying, 'You're looking well,' and, 'You don't alter a bit.' They were right. I had been very lucky.

During the next winter I was sawing up wood in the garden. Like a fool I slipped. It was back to my old clumsy ways. The saw gashed my finger. I began to panic. It was then I realized something uncanny was going on. I was frightened. It was weird. I had caught my finger with a sharp saw. I knew I had. You see, there was no mark. There was no cut, no blood. I knew what I had to do. I just had to go to the car. As I went indoors to get the keys, I slipped on some ice by the back door. I came down with a crack. I banged my forehead on the top step. It was a real crunch.

I was really scared now. I was really frightened. You know why, don't you? I couldn't feel a thing. There was no lump, no bruise, no headache, nothing. What I feared most now was what I would find in the garage. The Morris Minor had been fine when I put it away the night before. I opened the garage door. When I saw the car I felt sick. The windscreen was shattered but there was something else, something more horrible. I looked at my finger again — nothing. Then I looked down at the floor. Trickling out from under the car was thick dark oil — just like blood!

7

I thought I would tell someone about the car and how it got damaged when I hurt myself. It was daft. The more I thought about it, the more it seemed unreal. How could it possibly happen? It may just happen by chance. Perhaps I was imagining it all. How could I be sure?

I thought I would try to tell my friend, Paul. He was keen on my Morris Minor. He was interested in old cars. So I talked to Paul and he set me thinking.

'You've had that car a long time, haven't you?' he said. Paul was right. It was nine years since Uncle Bob had died. 'Well if you ever want to get rid of it, just let me know. I'll buy it from you.' I suddenly felt sick. The thought of getting rid of my Morris Minor made me feel ill. How could I? I could never part with it.

That started me thinking. I had not thought of getting rid of it before. It had never entered my head. It didn't seem right. I kept thinking about it. I began looking at other cars. A new car would be nice. I could afford one now. No, I couldn't think about it any more. My old faithful Morris Minor — I couldn't part with it after all these years.

Besides, there was still the mystery. I was sure the car was special.

I tried to explain to Paul about my finger and the oil and the windscreen. It all sounded so daft now. I could hardly believe it myself. I didn't say much more. He didn't take much interest. I don't think he understood.

I tried not to think about what had happened. I carried on driving the car as usual for another year or so. I was busy at work and at home in the garden. I was building a new garden wall. One evening as it was getting late I was just going indoors from working on my wall when a pile of bricks fell from the top. It could have been dangerous. I was lucky. They crashed to the ground but I got out of the way — all except my foot, that is. Some bricks fell with a thud on my right foot. I thought I had broken some toes.

It was then I felt fear again. Real fear. There was no pain. I hadn't thought about the car for a while. I knew I had to look at it. My foot didn't bother me at all. A pile of heavy bricks had just crashed on to it and ripped open my shoe. I went to the garage. Sure enough, it was as I expected, as I feared. The back tyre was flat, torn apart. It was on the right hand side.

15

8

You might think I was a fool. Why did I let a thing like this worry me? Well it did frighten me. I couldn't explain it. Things you can't explain can upset you, can't they? You might ask why I didn't go round doing what I liked, doing daring stunts all over the place. I couldn't get hurt. Well, I thought of that but it did frighten me. I don't like strange things I can't explain. Besides, if I did something to hurt me it cost a fortune to repair the car every time! I didn't like to think about it.

I went out to the garage and looked at the car. I just stared at it. I had owned that Morris Minor for over ten years now. Not much had gone wrong with it. I had looked after it. Somehow it was beginning to look its age. It actually looked as if it was getting old. I can't really put it into words. The car was clean and nothing was dented or broken. It still worked but somehow it seemed old and tired.

I still went to see Auntie Sue from time to time. She was beginning to look old. She still took an interest in the car. When I went round one time she was trying to paint the outside of the house. I told her she must let me do it. It wasn't a job for an old woman. I soon got on with it. I was just finishing it for her when I had an accident. I was up the ladder painting her window ledges white, when I slipped. I don't know how it happened, but I fell. I crashed to the ground with a thud. Paint went everywhere. Poor Auntie Sue was in the garden. She saw me do it. She saw me fall. It was a bad fall. She was shocked. She ran over to me. I was all right. She couldn't believe it. I was fine. I had fallen on my side but I was all right. I was so concerned about Auntie Sue getting upset that I forgot about myself — and about the car. She took me indoors and made some tea. 'I'm fine,' I kept telling her.

She soon calmed down and we began talking — about the old days and about Uncle Bob. 'It's strange,' she said, 'You have just had a nasty fall and you look fine. You look very well. You don't seem to have aged over the years at all. Why, you still look as young as you did when Uncle Bob taught you how to drive.' That made me think. Paul had said something like that the night before. I would soon be thirty but he said I still looked like a teenager. I suppose he was right. I did feel very young and fit. I had never been ill. Auntie Sue said something which interested me. 'You still look as young as you were in that photo.'

'Which photo is that?' I asked. 'The one Uncle Bob

took — on your first driving lesson. I keep it in that box over there. It was the last one he took. You can have it.' I hadn't seen it before. I went over to have a look. I soon found the photograph — the one with me sitting on the bonnet of the Morris Minor. Yes, it was true. I did look much the same as I did then.

I hadn't changed in all those years. The car had. It now looked so much older. But how could a car change? I went over to the window. I looked from the photograph in my hand, then out to the car in the road and back to the photograph again. Yes, there was something different, something weird. Suddenly I felt sick. I had forgotten all about my fall. The car reminded me. I couldn't believe it. Outside in the road, a long way from the house, stood my Morris Minor. The side was scratched and badly dented. I could see white splashes all over the roof of the car. It looked like white paint.

9

It cost a lot of money to repair the damage. The side of the car was dented, buckled and scratched. The white paint was hard to remove, too. It was all because of my fall. I was certain now. When I went to drive home, the car was battered. That photograph puzzled me too. I was just seventeen when it was taken. Why did I look the same now? It was funny. Most people can only dream of staying young, staying fit and never getting hurt. I could carry on like this for ever, I thought. My Morris Minor could grow old and get damaged for me while I would stay young and fit and have a good time. Yes, I began to like the idea. I was a fool. I didn't think of the other side of the coin. I had forgotten about that accident with the back bumper and how I had back ache. I was stupid. I began to drive carelessly. I thought no harm could come to me now. I could never get hurt. The car would take the damage.

Like a fool, I drove the car into my drive and didn't notice the dustbin was in the way. I drove straight into it. Smack. It went flying. I hit it with the front side of the car. There was a dreadful noise. Above all the clatter there was a scream. It was me.

My shoulder was broken. It was agony. My whole arm was grazed and scratched. I had dreadful bruises for weeks, all because of hitting that dustbin with the car. Of course, the car wasn't even scratched.

10

I became really frightened. What if something serious
happened to my car? I would be done for. This
power the car had over me was worrying. It was
fine when I was hurt and the car suffered, but I
didn't like it the other way round. I decided there
and then to lock the car up in the garage for good
and never get it out. That way it would be safe —
and so would I. It couldn't get damaged and neither
could I. I would lock it up so it couldn't get stolen.
That would be terrible. What would happen then?
I began to panic about what might happen. No, I
was sure. If that car was locked up safely in the
garage and never used, we would both be fine. I
was wrong.

I bought a new car. Well the Morris Minor was no
use to me now. What good was an old car kept
locked up in the garage? I needed one I could use.
I never went inside the garage. I almost forget
about my old car. It was Paul who reminded me.
It was Paul who told me I was looking older. 'Are
you all right?' he asked, 'You look ill.' He was right.
I did feel tired. I had lost weight. I was pale and
thin. I couldn't eat very much and I stayed indoors
all the time. I had no energy. I felt as though I

was slowing down, seizing up. All my joints were stiff. It was not easy to move. Of course, it made sense. I was a fool not to realize sooner. Paul said it straight away. 'You're getting like that Morris Minor of yours, out of condition. It must be seizing up just stuck in the garage all day. I wish you'd let me buy it.' Of course, that was why I was feeling weak and useless. It was the car.

What could I do? If I carried on like this I wouldn't last till my birthday next month. I would be thirty. I looked older than thirty now. I should have kept the car in perfect condition. It was too late now. I felt too ill to bother. I couldn't do any work on the car feeling like I did.

'I'd give you a good price for it. They're worth a lot now, you know.' Paul was still keen to buy my Morris Minor. Maybe that was the answer. That could end my problem. He would work on the car and restore it. He would look after it. The car might begin to affect him then. At least I would be rid of the problem. Yes, that was the answer. I should have thought of it before. I would sell it. 'All right then,' I said, 'It's yours, Paul.'

11

I didn't want much money for the car. Why hadn't I thought of it sooner? The moment Paul came to collect the car I felt much better. It needed a lot of cleaning, dusting and oiling. At last, after a lot of hard work, he got the car going again. He drove it away and I was glad. I had to smile. I was soon feeling fine. I had saved myself. I wondered how the car would affect Paul. Would the same happen to him? That would be his problem now. It was out of my hands.

I felt much stronger now. The Morris Minor was back on the road and so was I. The Morris Minor was working well again and so was I. We had both recovered.

In a way I was glad Paul had the car. I would still see it from time to time. That car had been in the family for many years. In fact, I wouldn't see it now till I was over thirty. I arranged a birthday party at my house. It was to be on the Saturday after my birthday. Paul was coming. He would bring the Morris Minor. I would see it again then. At least, that was what I thought. That was what I hoped. In fact, I will never see Paul again. I will

never see the car again. I won't live past my
birthday.

12

It is my birthday today. One minute I was fine and the next minute, I fell to the floor. I felt as if someone had beaten me up. My legs hurt, my arms hurt, my body hurt. Worst of all was the pain in my head. What had happened to me?

I felt so ill that I went straight to bed. I thought I would be better in the morning. But I wasn't. I felt the same, in fact I was worse. I dragged myself downstairs. I had to phone the doctor. I felt sick and ill inside. I felt as if I was falling apart. I had never felt so strange before. How could I explain to the doctor? I looked in the mirror. I looked really old. I looked much older than thirty. What was happening? What was going wrong? It was all to do with that car.

That photograph of me on the bonnet of the car was beside my bed. I just stared at it for ages, then picked it up. I saw something on the back. I hadn't seen the faint writing on the back before. There were four words in pencil. I could only just read them – 'Beware the Morris Minor'. I sighed. What did this mean? Perhaps it had been written by Uncle Bob. Had he known something about the car? It was all so strange. I could hardly move.

As I lay there in bed with that photograph in my hand, I sank into a deep sleep. The hours slipped away and my dreams were filled with fears. Would I wake up for my birthday? Would I get better? Night came, and the dull ache all through my body made me groan out loud in the darkness.

13

This morning my birthday cards arrived. I have slept since yesterday morning. I just about managed to open all my cards. The last one was from Paul. There was a short note inside. It said: 'Good news and bad news. Good news is I'll be bringing your present to the party on Saturday. Bad news − the car you sold me . . . it didn't last long I'm afraid. I had a bit of a smash up. To cut a long story short, the car is a write-off. I'll tell you all about it on Saturday.'

So that was it. It all made sense now. The car was on the scrap heap and so was I. He had crashed it. What would happen now? I dragged myself to the phone. I had to call Paul. He soon answered. It was true. He had crashed the car at the exact moment that I fell to the floor in pain. 'But what's going to happen to the car?' I asked. 'Please let me have it back. I must have it,' I pleaded. 'I'll pay you double.'

'Are you all right?' Paul asked. He could tell I was desperate. 'Sorry,' he said, 'it's too late. It was towed away. I was lucky to escape. It wasn't worth saving. It's going to be crushed up − made into scrap. They said they'd be doing it this afternoon

27

as a matter of fact. I'm sorry about it, but it will be a crunched-up box in a few minutes. That's the best thing for it.'

I was screaming. I was crying down the phone. It was too late. I put the phone down. It was no use. I had to face it. There was nothing I could do.

My body is a wreck. I can hardly move. I can only lie here and wait.

It is no use doing anything now. I can't stop my old Morris Minor being squashed to pulp. It is too late. When it is destroyed, I will be gone too. I feel my life is draining away. Any minute the crunch will come. First my uncle and now me. But I shall be the last . . . or shall I? What will happen to the scrap? What will become of my crunched-up car? I can't bear to think. What will become of me? Who will find me here, lying among my birthday cards?

I have said as much as I can. The tape recorder is beside me and the tape is turning. I will die but my story is safe on the tape. You must believe it. It has all happened. My voice is trembling. The tape is coming to an end. I must try to switch off and wait — just wait. There is nothing more to tell . . . .

A complete list of Spirals

Stories

Jim Alderson
Crash in the Jungle
The Witch Princess

Jan Carew
Death Comes to the Circus

Susan Duberley
The Ring

**Keith Fletcher and
Susan Duberley**
Nightmare Lake

John Goodwin
Dead-end Job

Paul Groves
Not that I'm Work-shy
The Third Climber

Anita Jackson
The Actor
The Austin Seven
Bennet Manor
Dreams
The Ear
A Game of Life or Death
No Rent to Pay

Paul Jennings
Eye of Evil
Maggot

Margaret Loxton
The Dark Shadow

Patrick Nobes
Ghost Writer

Kevin Philbin
Summer of the Werewolf

John Townsend
Beware of the Morris Minor
Fame and Fortune
SOS

David Walke
Dollars in the Dust

Plays

Jan Carew
Computer Killer
No Entry
Time Loop

John Godfrey
When I Count to Three

Nigel Gray
An Earwig in the Ear

Paul Groves
Tell Me Where it Hurts

Barbara Mitchelhill
Punchlines
The Ramsbottoms at Home

Madeline Sotheby
Hard Times at Batwing Hall

John Townsend
Cheer and Groan
The End of the Line
Hanging by a Fred
The Lighthouse Keeper's Secret
Making a Splash
Murder at Muckleby Manor
Over and Out
Rocking the Boat
Taking the Plunge

David Walke
The Bungle Gang Strikes Again
The Good, the Bad and the Bungle
Package Holiday